THE ADVENTURES OF COWGIRL AMY!

Cowgirl Amy and the Christmas Celebration

A Tradition Begins

Dr. Psalm

The Adventures of Cowgirl Amy!
Cowgirl Amy and the Christmas Celebration by Dr Psalm
Copyright © 2014 by Peace Psalm LLC
All Rights Reserved.
ISBN: 978-1-59755-282-0

Published by: ADVANTAGE BOOKS™
    Longwood, Florida USA
    www.advbookstore.com

This book and parts thereof may not be reproduced in any form, stored in a retrieval system or transmitted in any form by any means (electronic, mechanical, photocopy, recording or otherwise) without prior written permission of the author, except as provided by United States of America copyright law.

November October 2014
14 15 16 17 18 19 20 10 9 8 7 6 5 4 3 2 1
Printed in the United States of America

Cowgirl Amy and the Christmas Celebration

Dr. Psalm

"Halo and Howdy! My name is Cowgirl Amy! I love God, my family, friends, and my pony Slow Poke!

My Grandma Linda and I go on secret missions. We find God and praise in the most amazing places. Come and join us!

Today Grandma Linda is calling me for some help in celebrating Christmas with a new family tradition. She wears her yellow cowgirl hat when she needs my special Cowgirl Amy help.

Cowgirl Amy and the Christmas Celebration

Grandma Linda called me today on Skype. She was wearing her yellow hat, so I knew she needed my help. "Halo my Cowgirl Amy! How are you? I need your special Cowgirl Amy help!" said Grandma.

"Christmas is a special time when we celebrate the birth of the Lord Jesus Christ, and give thanks to God for giving His only son to us. I know you have some great traditions now. I need your help with a family tradition that allows me to celebrate with you over the telephone or on Skype.

Let's make a book to share our old and new favorite Christmas family traditions. We have a week and a day of traditions to put in our book!" said Grandma Linda.

'All right and Yee Haw! Let's get started!" I said.

THANKSGIVING

Grandma Linda said "Many families start the Christmas holiday celebration after Thanksgiving. Our family does this too."

I said, "Yes, we start playing Christmas music, and go on a hunting trip for a Christmas tree after Thanksgiving! Sometimes I dance, while I sing to the Christmas music. It is really fun!"

Grandma Linda replied, "Those sound like fun Christmas holiday traditions to keep and treasure!"

Thank you Heavenly Father for allowing us to celebrate You and Jesus with fun family traditions like Christmas music and Christmas tree hunting!

In the name of Jesus we pray, Amen!

Dr. Psalm

CHRISTMAS DAY COUNT DOWN! DAY 7

"A lot of families have an advent calendar that starts the Christmas count down on the first of December. Let's start our daily family Christmas traditions at the week countdown mark!" Grandma Linda said. "What shall we do on day seven?" she asked.

"I know! Let's draw names and make a prayer ornament for the person's name we draw! We can make them today and read them on Christmas Eve!" I said.

"What a great idea Cowgirl Amy! There are some clear plastic balls we may put the prayers in before we hang them on the tree. I really like this tradition, because you can read the prayers in person, by telephone or by Skype! This will be our new tradition!" said Grandma Linda.

"Yee haw! These will be fun to make!" I said.

I said "I want to say the prayer this time."

Grandma Linda said "That is awesome!"

Dear Father God, thank you for Your Son Jesus Christ. Thank you for the gift of prayer we share with family and friends.

In the name of Jesus we pray, Amen!

Dr. Psalm

CHRISTMAS DAY COUNT DOWN! DAY 6

"What shall we do on count down day six?" asked Grandma Linda.

"I know! Look for stars!" I said pointing to some stars.

"Wonderful idea Cowgirl Amy! The three wise men followed the Star of Christmas to find baby Jesus!" said Grandma Linda.

"Let's pray!" I said.

Dear heavenly Father, thank you for the stars that light up the night. Thank you for the Christmas star that kept baby Jesus in sight.

In the name of Jesus we pray, Amen

CHRISTMAS DAY COUNT DOWN! DAY 5

"Wow! Look at that Grandma Linda! There is a snow angel outside in front of the house! My mom, dad and I make them outside in the snow. We make some out of paper for inside too! I like this tradition!" I said.

Grandma Linda said "How fun! Snow angels make a great day five tradition. Angels were singing in the manger where baby Jesus lay in His cradle!"

I said "Let's pray!"

Dear Lord, thank you for angels that help look over us, and stood watch over baby Jesus!

In the name of Jesus we pray, Amen.

CHRISTMAS DAY COUNT DOWN! DAY 4

"How about day four? I know your mom and dad take you to see the live nativity before Christmas." said Grandma Linda.

"Yes! I get so excited to see it that I have to hold on to my hat!" I giggled.

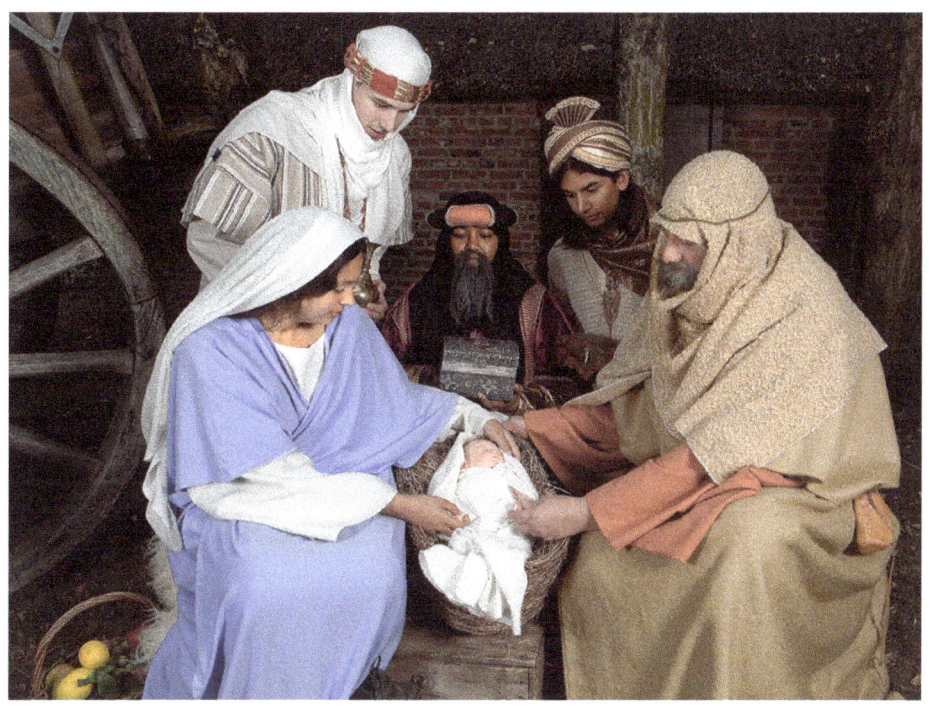

Dear Lord, thank you for people, who take the time to build and make live nativity scenes to remind us how special Jesus is to us.

In the name of Jesus we pray, Amen!

Dr. Psalm

CHRISTMAS DAY COUNT DOWN! DAY 3

"What happens on the day before Christmas Eve?" asked Grandma Linda.

"My mom, dad and I visit with friends and family, and we take treats to share the Christmas season with them! I really like visiting with my cousins, sharing Christmas cookies and singing Christmas songs! I am ready to go now!" I said.

"Sounds like fun! What a great way to celebrate Jesus! Let's pray before you go." said Grandma Linda.

Dear Lord, thank you for giving family and friends to us to celebrate the Christmas season! Thank you for tasty treats to share the joy of baby Jesus.

In the name of Jesus we pray. Amen.

CHRISTMAS DAY COUNT DOWN! DAY 2

"Christmas Eve! We have old and new traditions to share!" laughed Grandma Linda.

"Yes! Our old tradition is opening presents. I like to open presents! We pray before we open them. We thank God for giving baby Jesus to us and for the joy and presents we share to celebrate baby Jesus!" I said.

"Wow! That is a wonderful tradition!" said Grandma Linda.

"I like your new tradition of the prayer ball too! I made one and sent it to you!" said Grandma Linda.

"I know! I am excited to see what it says!" I said with a giggle.

"Let me share my prayer for you!" said Grandma Linda.

Dear Heavenly Father, thank you for blessing me with my wonderful granddaughter Cowgirl Amy! Your joy shines through her in her smile and laughter. She is a blessing and a gift.

In the name of Jesus we pray. Amen.

Dr. Psalm

CHRISTMAS DAY COUNT DOWN! DAY 1

"HAPPY BIRTHDAY JESUS!" I sang. "Yes, Christmas is a celebration of the birth of Jesus. I like the way you sing happy birthday in such a fun and loving way!

That is great Cowgirl Amy! I know that you and your mom make something special on Christmas morning." said Grandma Linda.

"Yes! We make birthday cupcakes and decorate them for Jesus' birthday. Then we sing happy birthday! I dance when I sing, because I am so happy to say happy birthday to Jesus!" I said.

"Let's pray." said Grandma Linda.

Dear Jesus!

HAPPY BIRTHDAY!

We love You and celebrate your birthday to honor YOU! In joy and praise we sing HAPPY BIRTHDAY TO YOU!

In Your name we pray. Amen.

Dr. Psalm

Sending Christmas prayers your way my friend!

I hope you liked our Christmas traditions, including our new prayer balls to share with Grandma Linda!

What are your traditions? I wish a Merry Christmas to you and your family!

Come and visit us next time for our Art Adventure! Grandma Linda is sending me on a secret mission to find a Bible book with clues in the museum artwork!

Until we meet again!

Your friend,

Cowgirl Amy

Dear Lord, thank you for my friends. Please watch over them and shower them with your love. May they feel Your love as they celebrate the birth of Your Son, Jesus Christ.

In the name of Jesus we pray. Amen.

Join Cowgirl Amy in her upcoming adventures!

- Cowgirl Amy and the Art Adventure
- Cowgirl Amy and the Texas Easter
- Cowgirl Amy and the Mystery of the Hidden Verses
- Cowgirl Amy and the Ranch at Christmas

Other adventures include:

- Cowgirl Amy and the Prayer Garden
- Cowgirl Amy and the Easter Adventure – A Tradition Begins
- Cowgirl Amy and Favorite Prayers for Mom
- Cowgirl Amy and Favorite Prayers for Dad
- Cowgirl Amy at the Cow Kid Zoo
- Cowgirl Amy and the Christmas Celebration – A Tradition Begins

SPECIAL THANKS TO:

Pipe Creek Christmas Tree Farm for allowing us to use the picture of their Christmas Tree Farm. Please support them and other farms that help families celebrate the joy of Christmas!

http://pipecreekchristmastrees.com/

Prayers, blessing and cheer!

Cowgirl Amy and the Christmas Celebration

For more information contact:

Dr Psalm
C/O Advantage Books
P.O. Box 160847
Altamonte Springs, FL 32716
info@ advbooks.com

To purchase additional copies of this book or other books published by Advantage Books call our order number at: 407-788-3110 (Book Orders Only)

or visit our bookstore website at: www.advbookstore.com

Longwood, Florida, USA
"we bring dreams to life"™
www.advbooks.com

Dr. Psalm

www.ingramcontent.com/pod-product-compliance
Lightning Source LLC
Chambersburg PA
CBHW042350040426
42449CB00018B/3479